NANA'S DIARIES

POEMS HE LEFT BEHIND AS MEMORIES.

NAVEEN GOVANI

ISBN 979-888606131-4

My cousin brother asked me if someone in the family wrote. As I am very insterested in writing and story-telling. Only my grandpa in my paternal family wrote thus he wanted to know if anyone in our maternal family did. I told him about the countless poems nana wrote and bhaiya said there is where I get my skills from. I scoffed at him and the light bulb went on! And here we are with a book published with Nana's poem.

We miss you Nana

Contents

1. Come Along.

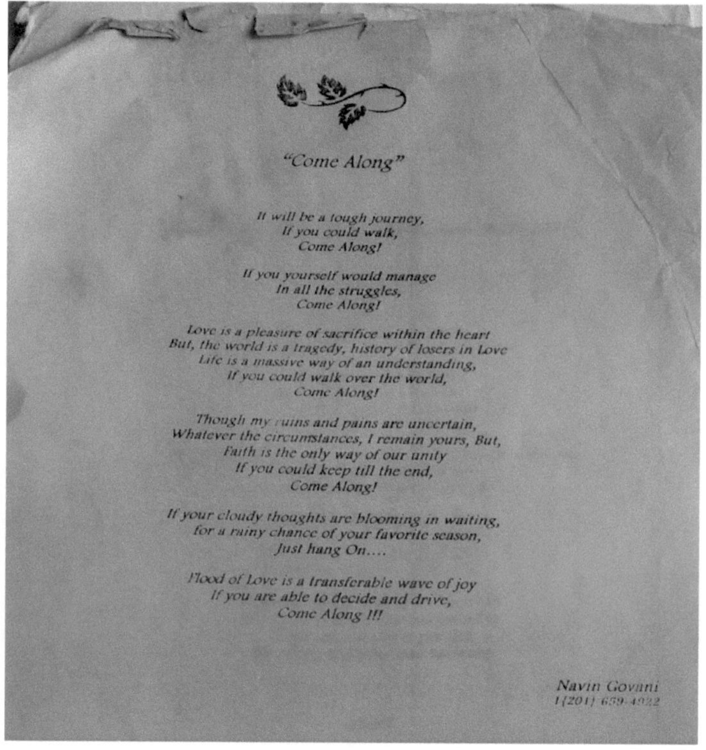

"Come Along"

It will be a tough journey,
If you could walk,
Come Along!

If you yourself would manage
In all the struggles,
Come Along!

Love is a pleasure of sacrifice within the heart
But, the world is a tragedy, history of losers in Love
Life is a massive way of an understanding,
If you could walk over the world,
Come Along!

Though my ruins and pains are uncertain,
Whatever the circumstances, I remain yours, But,
Faith is the only way of our unity
If you could keep till the end,
Come Along!

If your cloudy thoughts are blooming in waiting,
for a rainy chance of your favorite season,
Just hang On....

Flood of Love is a transferable wave of joy
If you are able to decide and drive,
Come Along !!!

Navin Govani
1(201) 659-4922

Nana loved writing about love. The passion for it was immense. He also was quite interested in business. A person who always wanted to stay fresh and never settle perhaps. He wrote about struggles, did he mean struggles of love? work? pain? who knows. This poem sounds like an invitation to join him in a new life leaving your old one. This new living is young, wild, and free in its very true essence. An invitation to leave the confusion, take a leap of faith, and drown in this flood of love. To endure the stresses of living and he assures us we have in ourselves to face the difficulties of life.

2. You Are Very Beautiful.

"You Are Very Beautiful"

No diamonds over neck
No jewelry over at all

No facial or face make up
Even though how beautiful
Your mighty simplicity
Is sweetie, beauty, beauty

Your hearty reality is
Pretty, Cutie, Cutie

How lovely, How truly?
How godly beautiful
You are very beautiful?

Your ever naturality
Is surety life warranty
Your super best quality
Is guaranteed eternity

How Vital? How Worthy?
How ever beautiful
You are very beautiful

Navin Govani

This poem has very little use of correct grammar but still stands out from the rest because of the very same reason. It seems like a 12-year-old kid who picks his nose in search of gold wrote this piece. It couldn't have been more innocent. It makes anyone blush because of the simplicity it exudes. And everyone likes some compliments thus it makes the reader warm at their heart. It indeed makes one feel beautiful. But sad news guys this poem isn't about us. It's about someone Nana loved dearly. Doesn't matter anyway. Its innocence leaves prints on the mind, which makes it beautiful.

3. Never Give Up.

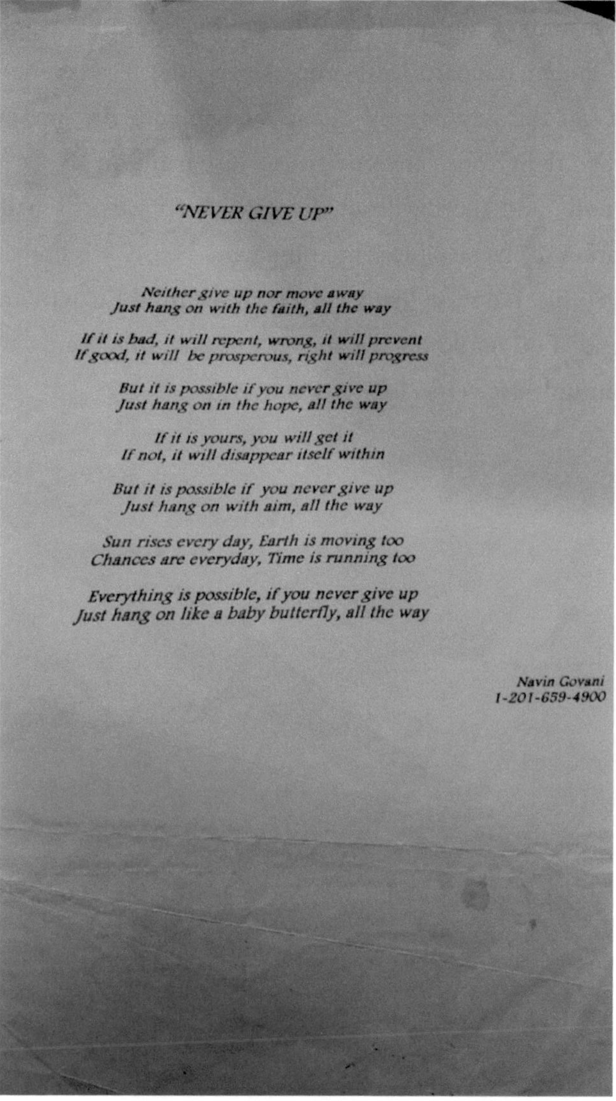

"NEVER GIVE UP"

Neither give up nor move away
Just hang on with the faith, all the way

If it is bad, it will repent, wrong, it will prevent
If good, it will be prosperous, right will progress

But it is possible if you never give up
Just hang on in the hope, all the way

If it is yours, you will get it
If not, it will disappear itself within

But it is possible if you never give up
Just hang on with aim, all the way

Sun rises every day, Earth is moving too
Chances are everyday, Time is running too

Everything is possible, if you never give up
Just hang on like a baby butterfly, all the way

Navin Govani
1-201-659-4900

Everyone's apparent favourite. This is one of rare nana's "motivational" poems. Hustle before hustle culture came in. This poem resonates with one as everyone has experienced that not the way in itself but us staying with the way made it the "right" one, once or twice. Just hang on like a little butterfly and the fog from the path disappears. Even if no solution seems possible something would arise. It is human to forget this. It'd seem like a miracle. It seems like magic, an act of god? I do not know the answer but one thing I am sure of is our universe works in pretty ways.

4. Love Yourself.

"LOVE YOURSELF"

Receive and have my rainy heart
your cloudy love does not wet your heart!
Use my heart as yours, and love yourself..
Treat your heart with my love, enjoy yourself!!!

My love, is yours and is with you forever,
Wherever you live, it will be your claim forever,

Don't work, if you don't love me. love yourself,
Thank you if you hate me, still you love yourself..

Whatever is your will and wish,
My choice is your love,
My love is your living hope...

Make your life free as before and love yourself
I want to see you innocent again,
Love Yourself

Look at my life as full of joy as a believer
My love grows in Jesus, who is my deliverer!!!

My concern is, regardless if you come to me or not,
Be with yourself!

Jesus is the only way, receive him to love yourself...

NAVIN GOVANI
1-800-659-4922

He tells a person to take his heart that loves them. For his heart loved them more than they do. He tells them not to worry about them not love themselves because him loving them satisfies his heart. He tells the person to love themselves to receive the love from Jesus. I'd like to add that while writing this commentary, I, unfortunately, couldn't add many poems because they were too complex for my understanding. I had to take out many poems that had the person and Jesus. Both were mentioned in the several poems. It is truly amazing how another could love us more than us sometimes. How unfortunate yet beautiful that is about the mordern human.

5. My Redeemer

"MY REDEEMER"

As your name has given me a new aim
Your love has made me a true wave of love..

The moment you enter into my heart, I firmly became
a true lover, which made me strong enough
to grow in faith and hope for my shaky love..

In the light of your righteousness, I remembered all my sins
and confessed before you at once..

Not only my sins were forgiven, but all the pains and ruins were
taken away as well as roots of the sins
also cut off, lusty eyes and dirty heart also were
cleaned by the holy blood and made me free…

When the devil struck me with a blow of death, as a massive stroke,
Lord, you poured a drop of your holy blood on the lips of my dead body,
I was raised to life!

Since you gave me a new birth with your holy blood
Lord, Jesus, Father Almighty blessed me eternity!!!

Na
1-800
201

Nana took up Christianity after survining a stroke. Which he wrote about in the end too. His love for Jesus had bloomed ever since. I remember my sister and I playing and troubling him while he read his prayers at night. When we tried to sleep while Pa went to pick Ma up from her office. His faith was boundless. He was grateful to the Lord for his healing. For blessing him. I love Nana's writing style though, full of vivid visual descriptions. I don't know if God exists. It could be that they don't but it's beautiful to see someone so in love. Hardly we see people with so much focus in something.

6. Loving Jesus

"Loving Jesus"

Since loving Jesus came
My life is changed already

So many years later, I saw
the flowers grow in my life

My heart is in love again
My soul is in joy again

Therefore, I sing this song
My life is changed already

Since loving Jesus came
My life is changed already

He gave me spirit of truth
With wisdom of an understanding

He gave me freedom of desires
with knowledge of righteousness

Therefore, this is my testimony
My life is changed already

Since loving Jesus came
My life is changed already

His blood circulates in my veins
His heart beats in my chest

He gave me the color of his blood
and support of his glorious name

Since he roused me from death,
My life is changed already

Since loving Jesus came
My life is changed already

This is another one of my favourite poems among his dozens of poems on Jesus. It seemed it had been a while he found joy. It was beautiful that faith can change someone's outlook this much. I hope we all have such accidents in life as he did thus having beauty in life. The simplicity of this poem speaks for itself. An explanation would not do justice to it. Simply beauty. Wisdom of understanding is indeed beautiful.

7. Why Haven't You.

"WHY HAVEN'T YOU"

Flower, Flower
Thirsty Beauty
You inspire me
Why haven't you come to me yet?
All the way, Surprising me…

I don't know, but, why should I know about you
When you don't know the truth in me
that I feel about you…

Love is a faith in my life,
Always helping me to survive
Why haven't you come to me yet?
All the way, Surprising me…

I will never give up hope,
My trust in Love,
In Our Love..
No matter what you think of me,
Try to believe - in our love…

If you don't understand me,
Never try to confuse me
No one can inconvenience me
Even if you refuse me…

Shower Days, Cloudy Days, Rainy Days
Wet weather or Lightening Days
No matter what the weather is..
I'm here for you, for us
Why haven't you come to me yet?
All the way, Surprising me…

This poem is awesome on its own. No commentary is needed perhaps.

8. My Wish.

"My Wish"

You rejoice all the time, it is a prayer of mine
I will suffer and survive
It is my last choice!

All my life I will be missing your presence
But, somehow, I will manage without you!

God will fulfill all your wishes and desires of your heart
You may keep yourself in good health, it is "my wish"

Lots of love you get from people around you
Everything to be given everywhere you do want

Be successful in every step whatever you plan for
Get a good name and hearty welcome wherever you go

Every night give you a good rest and sound sleep
Every day give you a lovely morning and healthy beginning

All the flowers do smile with you and give fragrance
All the waves of the breeze of springs play with your hairs

You enjoy your life as much as you like yourself
I will pray and keep praying for you from time to time!!!

ani
'900

He wishes someone to be happy while he manages with the void of their presence. He beautifully articulates what he feels for them. I wish Nana knew how the piano is played. This poem sounds like a warm song one would play on a summer's evening while gazing at the blue sky and looking at the clouds passing by.

9. Love Story.

"LOVE STORY"

There was a beautiful garden of flowers
The male and female parents were living there
Parets
This is a true Love-Story of those two love birds
I was told by the flowers, fragrances and the trees
The female was singing a sweet song as her heart was talking
The male was feeling shy, like most loving hearts feel in the beginning
hearts
The secret hears were hanging
into the hears, were not coming on lips
How long these growing facts could be hidden?
These are the truths coming out somehow!
One day, female found out that he male is in love with her
both of them then to inspired to become of each other forever

We shall live or die, but together! Togetherness became their desire

There was a beautiful garden of flowers
The male and female parents were living there
Parets
Then, all of a sudden one day, one human devil came to the garden
He took away the female parent and her lover was almost dying
The flowers were explaining about their sufferings of separation and telling
They were often singing that the nights are not ending without darling

"It was a beautiful atmosphere and tears were falling from eyes"
There was a beautiful garden of flowers,
The male and female parents were living there
Parets
They were hearing all the time, the voices of their souls
When did the love stop? By these worldly grown walls
Cannot even stop them, both, all the world or the god!
"Cage" was broke and birdie flee, devil too kept greeting

To sing the song again for her lover, she returned to the garden
Remember this story of "Living Love", forever
If you too have anybody, "Love", like these love birds!!
Love

Navin Govani

Hands down the best poem I've heard. This is a story inside a story. How pretty could it get? The fantasy of the parrots speaks of one another. Even though the spelling of parrots was wrong, the feeling was more than right. I guess it wasn't his mistake, the flowers who told him the story didn't know the word's spelling perhaps. Shyness and singing are the beginning of this love. Then came togetherness, Then the separation which filled the atmosphere with salty and humid airs of tears. Breaking the restraints of the unloving world the birds found back to each other. Nana dares lovers to love like them.

10. Wherever.

"WHEREVER"

Wherever you got to go
feel me there with my love
see my face everywhere

"Wherever you got to go"

Every thought will speak my story
love makes beautiful memories
Anywhere you try to go
hear my words of love song
in your heart at all times

"Wherever you got to go"

However, we dwell in each other
as two souls blessed by the Creator
Whatever you choose to do
See my life in your eyes
let it grow by your love

"WHEREVER YOU GOT TO GO

"As two souls oblessed by the very creator", reminds me of listening to Prateek Kuhad's songs. Like slow guitar, this poem plays with hearts. The lover in the poem does wish the very best for the other. In baked cakes, a pinch of salt is added to make them delicious. The contrast of the sweetness in the batter with the saltiness makes the poem even more melancholic. The salt of the sadness of separation. Hoping that they love and miss us as much as we do. Naturally what one would feel after separating is what Nana seized in words.

11. My Seperate Village.

"My Separate Village"

Your picture is always hanging before my eyes
I have created a separate village from this world

There is nothing else in my heart except your love,
All I remember is your smiley, innocent face

You are away and already gone faraway, that,
You never even talked or met with me,
Since long ago

Yet, your words and voice are heard around my ears
I can feel and see you all the time within me

I understand nothing about neither past nor future,
All I know is that your are with me as Love and Love!

My songs will reach up to your lips one day
And we will have to sing together! I Promise!

Because your inspirations gave me a life and
I have created a separate village from this world!

This poem too is super simple to understand and thus is beautiful. No commentary is needed here too.

12. Good Bye To Everybody.

"Good-Bye To Everybody"

Navin Govani
3/99

Finally, I am going away soon
Good-bye to everybody, see you again!

Thank you very much for participating
Into my poetry journey so far!

You all heard and touched my heart
By joining and sharing my on goings!

I will remember every one of you
And try to visit through "Family Unity"

Please forgive me if I hurt anybody
Because I was in joy and pain together

May God be with you and
Bless you all for all your life!

May God fulfill all your wishes
And give you peace and joy together!

Since, I am going away soon
Good-bye to everybody
See You Again!

This is wholesome for a "good-bye" message. It was difficult for me to comment on this because of hoe straightforward this poem is. I tried my best. This sounds like something someone would say when they're going away forever. And if Nana wanted this to be his last message, I'd surely understand. The heart-warming message it tries to put across is just wonderful. We surely miss you!

13. My Life Poetry.

"My Life Poetry"

I may become a poet someday
In your love my life poetry

I keep remembering you again and again
I found you even in my dreams and visions

I looked often and often in my heart,
and saw the love overflowing for you and you

I may become your heart beat one day
In your love my life poetry

I find you also as the window of my love memory
You may be also thinking about our love-story

Your love is my living light and all inspirer
I keep you in my prayers as you are my desire

I may become your favorite any day
In your love my life poetry

I may become a poet some day
In your love my life poetry

Navin Govani

"In your love my life poetry." tells the truth about nana writing the end number of poems for that one person. He misses that person dearly. Prays for them and hopes to become their favorite someday. Helplessly being reminded of them shows his endless devotion to them. Their love is an inspiration and a window of their love memory. Hoping even after separation they miss him and his story. Praying for them and their love being his only inspirer. Hoping to become a poet someday for them.

14. Mother

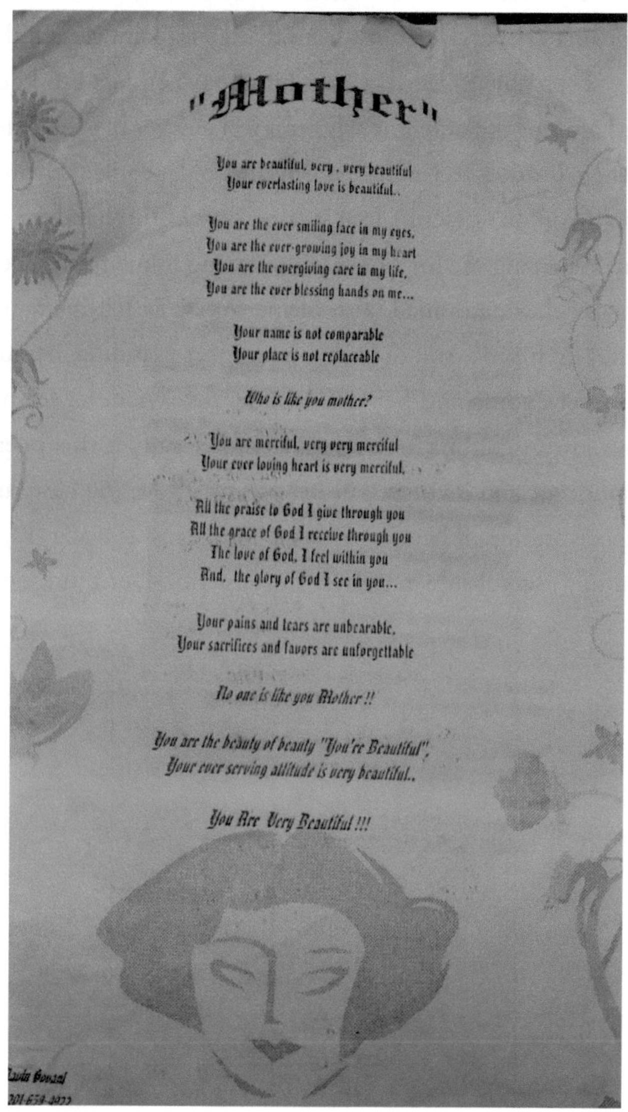

"Mother"

You are beautiful, very , very beautiful
Your everlasting love is beautiful..

You are the ever smiling face in my eyes,
You are the ever-growing joy in my heart
You are the evergiving care in my life,
You are the ever blessing hands on me...

Your name is not comparable
Your place is not replaceable

Who is like you mother?

You are merciful, very very merciful
Your ever loving heart is very merciful,

All the praise to God I give through you
All the grace of God I receive through you
The love of God, I feel within you
And, the glory of God I see in you...

Your pains and tears are unbearable,
Your sacrifices and favors are unforgettable

No one is like you Mother !!

You are the beauty of beauty "You're Beautiful",
Your ever serving attitude is very beautiful..

You Are Very Beautiful !!!

This was written for Nana's mom or my great-grandma who I unfortunately never met but from the poem, I am certain that I have been able to learn quite a bit about her. Glad to know that I am not the only one who can feel an ever blessing hand on their head. I feel nana's warm and old people's smelling (sorry I couldn't describe it any other way LOL!) hand on my head. Caressing me for I have come crying home from school after my classmates made fun of me. As Nana felt his mom's hand, I do his too, still do. Oh, about great-grandma, her love was never-ending and her care wonderous. We never learned about great-grandma and pa ever before reading this poem. As innocent and loving as all his poems. I love the clear and simple wordings of Nana's writings. Unlike mine, using "high-sounding" words just to express I'm superior. Don't judge me.

Printed by Libri Plureos GmbH in Hamburg, Germany